# Down the Dog Hole

## 11 Poets on Northeast Pennsylvania

Edited by

Thomas Kielty Blomain

and

Brian Fanelli

NIGHTSHADE PRESS
Keystone College • La Plume, PA

Nightshade Press is an imprint of Keystone College.

Nightshade Press
Keystone College
One College Green
La Plume, PA 18440

www.keystone.edu

Copyright © 2016 by Keystone College

Copyright of individual works are retained by their authors.

All rights reserved. No part of this book may be used or reproduced in any manner whatsoever without written permission of the author except in the case of brief quotations embodied in critical articles and reviews.

First Edition

Set in Calibri

Layout and Design by Raymond P. Hammond

Cover Art by Mikayla Lewis, Keystone College Class of 2017

Proofread by Kimberly Boland, Keystone College Class of 2017

Nightshade Press Logo by David W. Porter

Library of Congress Control Number: 2016913837

ISBN: 978-1-879205-92-5

# Down the Dog Hole

# Contents

Preface   / xi
Introduction   / 17

## The Museum of a Scranton Morning
*poems by Thomas Kielty Blomain*

View of Scranton in Winter   / 25
Metaphor of an Old Man   / 26
Forgetting John Mitchell   / 27
Watching the Past Repeat Itself   / 28
The Museum of a Scranton Morning   / 30

## Polluted Sunsets
*poems by Amanda J. Bradley*

Polluted Sunsets   / 35
City to Country   / 36
A Straight Shot   / 38
Ricketts Glen   / 39

## Cemetery Overlooking the Stripping Pit
*poems by Craig Czury*

It seemed like...   / 43
Softest grass, edgiest...   / 44
Between the river...   / 45
Because the men...   / 46
You know, butt,...   / 47

## Space and Time
*poems by Erin Delaney*

Reflections on the Remains of the Ashley Coal Breaker   / 51

Space and Time:  @StationCDRKelly   / 52

Thirst   / 53

Mortality and the Uncut Rock   / 54

## Transparency
*poems by Nancy Dymond*

Transparency   / 57

Under a Small Town:  Two Conversations   / 58

Make New Friends   / 60

Measured by Mercury   / 62

## Night Music
*poems by David Elliott*

Again   / 65

Through the Air   / 66

Rain in Nicholson   / 67

Climate   / 68

Night Music   / 69

### *Surviving Winter*

*poems by Brian Fanelli*

Outside a Scranton Deli, Talk of War   / 73
Evacuation   / 74
Autumn at Home   / 76
Surviving Winter   / 77
Steamtown Mall, Scranton   / 78

### *Cold Comfort*

*poems by Jane Julius Honchell*

Expendable   / 81
Travelers' Advisory   / 82
Joy Ride   / 83
Cold Comfort   / 84

### *The Sharing*

*poems by Susan Luckstone Jaffer*

Tara Hall   / 87
Dream: February 12, 2002   / 88
The Visit   / 90
The Sharing   / 91
A Pantoum for Gillian   / 92

***The River***
───────────────────────────────────────────────
*poems by Dawn Leas*

Susquehanna   / 95
The River   / 96
A Lesson on Resilience   / 97
Independence   / 98
Storm Front   / 99

***Stages of Forgiveness***
───────────────────────────────────────────────
*poems by Laurel Radzieski*

Mine Story I   / 103
Mine Story II   / 104
Mine Story III   / 105
Stages of Forgiveness   / 106

Acknowledgments   / 107
About the Authors   / 111

# *Preface*

The idea for this volume came up, appropriately, in Zummo's, a nice little café in the Green Ridge section of Scranton, Pennsylvania. When I was a kid, Zummo's was both a penny candy store and a shoe repair shop, side-by-side. I still smell Red Hot Dollars and Kiwi wax as soon as I open the door to the place. Right across the street is St. Paul's School, and the church where I learned how to manufacture confessions and dramatize penance—ultimately valuable skills for a poet. The entire neighborhood resonates for me in sacred ways that have little to do with the religion that seemed, to me as a boy at least, to be at its center. Maybe that's always the way it is with our childhood turf; that a deeper reverence for it develops the further away from it we get in life. It is the place with the oldest echoes.

As Brian Fanelli, Ray Hammond, and I sat there over coffee one morning, talking about poetry and world problems, the notion evolved to produce an anthology built around the loose theme of our region, its landscape, environment, and history, showing different perspectives and poetic personalities. Ray, a relative newcomer to the area, was fascinated by the concept of a "dog hole." It dug into his imagination, spurring him to blast out the title. Bringing his editorial expertise to Nightshade Press from years experience with the legendary *New York Quarterly,* and studying with its renowned founder, William Packard, Ray's sonic love for poetry and publications collide in this volume. His vision for the future of Nightshade Press includes sculpting a mission of publishing literature born from—but transcending—regionalism. This book jumps toward that idea.

Brian and I were decreed co-editors. Between us, we've persisted through a litany of literary arts endeavors, throughout our region and beyond, including Mulberry Poets and the Writers Showcase, to name just two connections. We decided to seek out submissions from a cross-section of poets who live and work in the region, some long-timers—the usual suspects—and some newer voices. I believe we have struck a nice balance here, both stylistically and thematically, accomplishing the worthy goal of producing an important, yet highly readable, anthology of new poetry.

A couple of lines from Rilke's *Letters to a Young Poet* that have long influenced me asserted themselves as we considered the direction of this production. He wrote: "There is much beauty here, because there is much beauty everywhere." Obviously, he didn't mean northeastern Pennsylvania specifically, but that there is beauty wherever you are and it is your own obligation to see it. Nor was he necessarily referring to "beauty" as an essence of loveliness. I believe he was stretching the common definition of "beauty," the way a poet should force us to crawl through breaches in our understanding of things. He also wrote: "Everything you can think of in the face of your childhood, is right." This struck me like a nun's ruler, as we sat there in Zummo's and I looked across Marion Street toward my red brick childhood school/reformatory.

There are some things you never get past. They never go away, and they are valuable because they keep you honest to yourself. For those of us brought up in the paradox of Scranton, there is glory in the sooty grit that stays with you, a humble kind of hubris, an enigmatically haughty modesty, in which even our delusions of grandeur are less grand than they should be. It is something that no one who lived here as a child ever escapes. It is a feeling that "the least incident unfolds like a destiny," as Rilke wrote. It is as deep and dark as a mine shaft, and as bright as the light at the end of the tunnel. It is the origination of sound and its echo.

For this book, we chose to go with eleven poets, not for any special reason other than it seems enough to provide a fair sample of work touching on the theme. Eleven is also an odd number, which seems somehow significant. Some of the poets in this book I've known for a long time; others, I've only gotten to know lately. The arc of time is confounding in the bloodline of poetry. What happened yesterday was really twenty years ago, and last week is so long past. But poetry transcends chronology and geography. These "place poems" are a portal, a way to witness the flow of change, to challenge your view of beauty, and also to participate in history. Whether you have lived in northeastern Pennsylvania your whole life or have never even driven through, the monuments that fill these pages are worth your attention. Enjoy your visit.

—*Tom Blomain*

# Down the Dog Hole

*Introduction*

It is an honor and privilege to present this anthology of poems, *Down the Dog Hole,* focusing on the environment, culture, and history of northeastern Pennsylvania. One of the aims of this project is to showcase the wide range of literary talent in this region. While this anthology was created with a particular theme in mind, the poems are diverse in range, form, and subject matter.

In Tom Blomain's opening poem, "View of Scranton in Winter," his unrhymed tercets present two images that are a fixture to this area—a Catholic church and winter. Another one of his poems, "Forgetting John Mitchell," ensures that Mitchell and his involvement in the Scranton coal strikes and labor negotiations is not forgotten. Blomain's poems are rooted not only in Scranton history, but also its neighborhoods, such as Courthouse Square and Penn and Capouse Avenues.

Other poems are more particular to man-made environmental crises. Amanda J. Bradley's poem, "Polluted Sunsets," presents an apocalyptic future caused by global warming. The poem concludes, "Now I imagine we will get our own time capsules/emblazoned down the sides with our names. We will shoot/them into gorgeous, polluted sunsets on rockets/ as we become piles of ash with no one to remember us anyway." Another one of Bradley's poems, "City to Country," juxtaposes the grit and grime of living in New York City with the gorgeous Endless Mountains of this region. That said, the poem is not without a moral, pointing out how few people in the countryside recycle, due to the cost.

Craig Czury's five prose poems recall abandoned mine shafts and kids entering them, spinning rumors about what they found or imagined that they found. Erin Delaney's poem, "Reflections on the Remains of the Ashley Coal Breaker," also acknowledges this region's previous powerhouse industry, and, like Blomain's "Forgetting John Mitchell," it is steeped in history. Delaney's poem, however, looks at what remains decades after the coal industry folded. Her poem speaks of "abandoned coal crushers and factories," "thick, broken windows," and "empty executive desks" with expenditures dated from years ago.

Other poems celebrate the simple beauty of this area and some of the small towns that surround Scranton and Wilkes-Barre. Nancy Dymond's poems have references to the Bluebird Diner in Factoryville and Skinners Falls. Her poems are filled with small town culture and conversations. David Elliott's poem, "Again," centers around the image of ducks flying through the sky and the speaker's connection and reaction to it. Another one of Elliott's poems, "Rain in Nicholson," jokes about how much it rains in the rural town.

Jane Honchell's poem, "Expendable," takes the theme of mining that is an undercurrent in this book, but does something unique with it, asking the reader to imagine his or her son as a breaker boy, descending the mines in Olyphant or Carbondale, working 10-hour days, or longer, for only 50 cents. Honchell's poems are not without humor, however. Her poem "Travelers' Advisory" opens with the lines, "If you are a deer reading this/first let me say: Stay away!" Yet, Honchell acknowledges that there is something majestic about the animals, despite some of the havoc that they cause on I-81 or Route 6. She concludes the poem, "your large/wild presence/just inches from my/window, makes me believe."

Susan Luckstone Jaffer's poems are set on farms and rural landscapes, populated with characters and personal memories tied to this region. The speaker in "The Sharing" continually encounters Emma Jean each fall, who asks her if she has any apples. The poem moves in and out of memory seamlessly. The speaker recounts her days heading out to the cider mill before autumn was "more than a doorway to dog dishes/frozen to the ground, ice underfoot, bleak and impassable roads." The poem pushes deeper, to the history between the speaker and the neighbor and their conversations over life tragedies, before the poem returns to the image of apples.

Instead of addressing what can feel like the endless northeast Pennsylvania winter, or some of the green summertime scenery, Dawn Leas showcases the force of the Susquehanna River, which flooded parts of Luzerne County in 1972 during Hurricane Agnes and then again in 2011 during Hurricane Irene. In her prose poem "Independence," the relentless rain that falls stands as a metaphor for a fragile relationship and the hint that it could end at any moment.

The anthology concludes with Laurel Radzieski's section "Stages of Forgiveness," which again leads the reader back down the dog hole, to the cavernous mines that are an undeniable part of this region's history and story. Her short prose poems, "Mine Story I," "Mine Story II," and "Mine Story III," highlight the dangers of the mines, including cave-ins, while her final poem, "Stages of Forgiveness," speaks of a "father," who could be a literal character or a stand-in for the mining industry and its relationship to this area and all of us still living in its shadow.

*Down the Dog Hole* is meant to celebrate the northeastern Pennsylvania region and illustrate the many facets of its environment, history, and culture. These poems address everything from the John Mitchell-led labor strikes and negotiations with President Teddy Roosevelt in Scranton, to the devastation caused by Hurricane Agnes and Hurricane Irene, to the small town conversations happening every morning at the Bluebird Diner. Most of all, this book showcases how alive this literary community is and how the rich and storied history of this region is continually an inspiration to all.

—*Brian Fanelli*

# *The Museum of a Scranton Morning*

*poems by Thomas Kielty Blomain*

## View of Scranton in Winter

The houses kneel in avenue pews
  The rooftops like the lined hands of children
    Folded to point skyward for their required prayers

Clouds are puffs of harsh incense
  From a gilded censer swung
    On the loud chain of a hard past

Stained glass icicles hang from eaves
  As the tithe basket of dawn passes to night
    The hymns of another winter echo

In all the voices that make no sound
  The windows maw like open mouths
    The souls of these hopeful congregants

Yearning to be heard
  Not just as a confession to a forgetful god
    But as a testament to the rest of the world

        —*Thomas Kielty Blomain*

# Metaphor of an Old Man

The side streets in Scranton tell the best stories,
The little courts and alleys between avenues,
Where the tilted houses help hold each other up,
Their rambling narrative like an old man who sits
In a folding chair on a chipped-paint porch, full of long pauses

At dusk, when the city drips from the sky's gray palette,
There are the hands of someone who has touched it all,
Someone touched by everything but the one thing
That remains unsaid at each sentence's end

I've pulled up beside him on a thousand worn seats,
Leaned in to bring my ear close to his pursed lips,
Almost rasped by the coarse whiskers of his cheeks,
Waiting to hear his final admission of despair

But it never comes.
Instead, he laughs loudly, gruffly, leaning back,
Not caring one bit about who laughs with him

When he points something out, you can tell
By the knuckles he's worked hard, and the words he uses
To explain how he came to be precisely where he is today
Fail to portray any notion of remorse. Of course, he wishes
He had more money, but he quickly shrugs that demon away

As night falls, the lone lamppost out front bestows a halo
Over the cramped neighborhood. He blesses himself
Unconsciously—more in defiance than subservience—
Hearing an ambulance go by

As the siren gets louder the closer it comes,
He remembers some of the wild times he's had
And breaks into a vast, crooked smile

*—Thomas Kielty Blomain*

## Forgetting John Mitchell

Once they built the highway around the town,
Travelers could bypass the rows of kneeling houses,
Avoiding the black mountains
Left along the roadsides like bad monuments
To the coal once dug out of this city's guts
Long ago to heat the homes of a new America,
Which quickly forgets its debts and moves on
To places less spent

The regrets of the mine owners were few.
Their sons and daughters went away to school,
Somewhere in Massachusetts or Connecticut,
Returning for obligatory visits to old family members
Who still live near the bland Episcopal church
Built out in the country long ago just to serve them

The grand Catholic cathedrals, scattered
Throughout the valley, with their hopeful spires
Poking up from the broken landscape,
Were all paid for in small change,
Coins that would otherwise buy
A Sunday meal or re-heel a worn pair of shoes

The view today is one of iron poles
Channeling wires across denuded hilltops
To bring light to distant vistas
Where neon signs call clean people
Into fine restaurants and stores, fueling
A future where a dirty past can easily be ignored

In Downtown Scranton, on Courthouse Square,
There is a statue to the leader of the miners,
Who, but only a century ago, saved children
From the hell of their expendable fathers,
Still there with his bronze hand held out,
While the rest of us go on about our business,
Of forgetting and forgiveness,
As if history has only to do with the past

—*Thomas Kielty Blomain*

## Watching the Past Repeat Itself

The red brick schoolhouse,
Between the avenues of Penn and Capouse,
Still churns well dressed children out

Now I watch from a coffee shop across Marion Street,
Which used to be a candy store and shoe repair,
Back when I was one of these children here

Making mild mischief until the nuns swooped in,
Behind the place where they tore
The old convent down over there

It was heroic glory back then to climb the culm bank
After school, where we'd stand over the neighborhood
Like dirty little lords covered in the soot

Of our forbidden conquest. We'd smoke the cigarettes
We stole from the pharmacy, and laugh at rules
Few really followed, before heading home

To certain punishment. This is how we learned
To be careful not to get caught playing in the waste
Of the universe we were graced to be born into

There was something thrilling about reaching the top,
Scratching your way up through the slag that boys our age
Once cracked off with their bare hands to build this hill

Today, though, that black mountain is gone,
Like the convent, and the past. Only the school still stands,
And the church, with a newly paved parking lot in between

And those uniformed boys I see, in the very same place
Where we used to concoct our little schemes.
Everyone has high hopes for them

Including me. But I do feel sorry for the loss
Of the kind of dangers they don't have anymore.
All their concerns have changed to numbing fears

In this new world. Yet I have to smile as I watch them,
Beating now with sticks they found
Against the side of a dumpster like a drum

  —*Thomas Kielty Blomain*

# The Museum of a Scranton Morning

There are mornings here I wouldn't trade
For any fancier place, especially in January,
When the sepia tone of cold mountains
Portrays an old family photograph, only
Different because the people are missing

Deceased or moved away, they converse
With me still, in a language no one else understands,
The accent, untranslatable to others
Raised without the soot in their blood,
Common among those of us who have remained

Right out my back window, the old silk mill hunkers
In the dell just below the highway across this little valley,
Telling its quiet story of satin yearning to the congregation
Of bare trees, at least until the verbose sun comes up,
Preaching its impatient sermon again about moving on

But there really is no leaving, even if you go away,
Even if you reach your fingers into the distance
To grasp for home in another location,
There is still the magnetic song of crows
Who will always love it here

If only for those things we've left on the roadside.
We will forever see them in our rearview mirrors,
As we drive from the houses, whose rooftops
Look like hands folded in prayer, built before
Everything changed, and we sold ourselves

On the bleak notion that dreams only come true
In cities where the sidewalks are clean,
And that museums are places to visit
But not somewhere to live.
And between all of it

I continue to try to squeeze myself in
To this exhibit, a curious facet of a diorama
That moves, but so slowly that those who wander by
And merely glance over the scene may barely ever see
That there is any change at all

*—Thomas Kielty Blomain*

# *Polluted Sunsets*

*poems by Amanda J. Bradley*

## Polluted Sunsets

The new neighbor deemed them "redneck wind chimes,"
but the loose tiles dangling from the house next door
shake a haunting, irregular tune. I imagine keys on a piano
as in *Eyes Wide Shut* as I suffer in the summer heat.
I believed we were killing the planet long ago but trusted
I would not live to see its early death throes. I worried
I would not write enough good poems to be remembered.
Now I imagine we will all get our own time capsules
emblazoned down the sides with our names. We will shoot
them into gorgeous, polluted sunsets on rockets
as we become piles of ash with no one to remember us anyway.

    *—Amanda J. Bradley*

## City to Country

Every night, I washed grime off my face
living in New York and Chicago. Exhaust
from cars, soot, and dust gathered
on my skin in nearly visible layers.
Summers in New York, piles of trash bags
as tall as me full of broken eggshells stuck
with stinking yolk, wilted lettuce, cartons
lined with swaths of spoiled milk stood
along sidewalks, their stench blasting
the air as cars blew by. But recycling
was the law. Cops lifted bags of trash
listening for the clink of glass, knocked
on doors to uncover violators. Friends
baked in hot apartments refusing to
use air conditioners that would emit
chlorofluorocarbons to deplete ozone.
In the shadows of vaulting skyscrapers
built by magnificent minds and careful
hands scurried people who cared to slow
climate change, ducked into holes
to board trains beneath the earth
because they did not own cars.

Now I live in the Endless Mountains of
northeast Pennsylvania, where the vast
green of treetops dots valleys and peaks
as we drive curving roads cut into
the sides of hills beneath the blue dome
that appears more blue here, where
autumn blossoms in violent bursts
of red, orange, yellow, and I almost
believe again. But no one recycles.
It is difficult and expensive. You must
save bags for weeks, stinking up your
kitchen or basement or haul overflowing
bags to bins miles away. This is fracking

country, and the natural gas companies
pay for the water jugs delivered
to homes. No one can trust their water.

Some days, gazing at the glory of
the Susquehanna winding alongside
the road beside me as I drive,
its power and movement undulating
with such authority, a great fear
wells up within me that we have
already as good as lost this beauty.

—Amanda J. Bradley

# A Straight Shot

As I sit on the deck behind the house
trying to pull a new voice from the bellows,
I hear little syncopated whiffs of wind
then thuds against what I turn to discover
is a target. There's a young man shooting
a BB gun. I've seen him before and ducked
inside to avoid stray pellets I imagined
tagging me in the eye or shooting
through my ear into my brain. I read
Kurt Vonnegut's *Deadeye Dick* at thirteen.
In it, a woman vacuuming her home
is hit by a ricocheting bullet. We are to take
from this the desultory habits of fate,
the fact that we could kick at any moment.
Carpe diem if you can. Smoke 'em if you
got 'em. I have tried to balance long views
with these facts of death. What strikes
me now is how his world is so completely
his own, discrete. He wants to be a straight shot
for his reasons cooked up by his mind as part
of his world, his vision. And I sit here sounding
like myself, drinking bitter beer in the sun
as I do, trying hard to sound like that other
person I am convinced is within.

—Amanda J. Bradley

## Ricketts Glen

My brother is in town for a few days, has brought furniture
for our new home from Indiana. He looks up hiking in the area.
It has never occurred to me to do so. I pull my brown Nine West
boots that look like hiking boots to me from my closet for the
adventure. We pick the seven-mile hike alongside waterfalls.
As we approach the base of the trail, I notice my feet are wet.
I pause and lift my left foot to observe the disintegrating sole
of what clearly are only hiking boots for show. It is difficult
to catch my breath on the trek back up the other side of the falls.
I leave pieces of my boots along the trail like breadcrumbs.

We have not eaten and are covered in dirt and sweat. We stop
for groceries. I try to recall the ingredients for white bean
chicken chili. He will make kale chips. At home, I realize I have
forgotten the broth and am unsure what to do. My brother,
pro chef, jokingly and dramatically tells me to "move aside."
A delicious impromptu meal is before us in fifteen minutes.

It has been an amazing day. I remember the pudgy kid he
was at eight who mean kids called "four eyes" and who
irritated me in the backseat of the car by crossing the
imaginary line between us to poke my shoulder. He is so
competent now—a father of three, a devoted husband,
the president of a successful company, particularly adept
at technology. I think how he built his own fishing boat,
how he made wine for a while, how he is a pro on the grill
and smokes one turkey at Thanksgiving. We sit on the
deck that night, and he tells me about recent scientific
discoveries, ideas he has for novels he wants me to write.
I want to reach over that imaginary line and poke his shoulder.

*—Amanda J. Bradley*

*Cemetery Overlooking the Stripping Pit*
___

*poems by Craig Czury*

**It seemed like** picker bushes wrapped around me, they were pulling me in. Then, I heard that noise again. It had dead birds and a dead cat in it. There was a sewing machine and bullet holes in the rusty car doors. The coal was hard on my shoes, and newspapers from 1937, only worse. Something was holding me back, but the door was open. There were no steps to get down there, only a broken window against the wall. We were sending messages over the pipe, but I couldn't get through. I was soaked and my shirt got ripped. It was near the cement city. There were chalk drawings and what looked to be a ribcage.

—*Craig Czury*

**Softest grass, edgiest** night to undress each other and seep into the moon wide air. Who more deserves this than the dead, boneyard softer than a golf green with its undulating mossy fingers. Ah, the acrobatics, draped around, against and over the headstones. Middle of the night grunting moans neighbor kids create legends from, tearing up into the next morning on their bikes. Look, the cloven footprints from your fingers stove into the ground from those crumbling limestone heights. The perfect circle of clover.

*—Craig Czury*

**Between the river** and the cemetery, I have a secret walk through the alleys no one knows. And if you saw me? I think I'm invisible, past the sleeping dog and dead squirrel. I take the trash route. I take the broken glass route. I take the rocks and rusted metal route, leaning against your beat-up car to empty my shoe. A phone rings inside a house. Hey, I'm a burn barrel back alley kinda guy, deflated and who knows where. I go looking for myself in your tires and overturned shopping carts. I am a runaway shopping cart with one good wheel rickety and wobbling toward hell knows where.

*—Craig Czury*

**Because the men** I grew up among had no childhood (an American invention since WWII), they had coal mines, textile mills, factories, wars... I wondered at what age would I become disapproving and dour. I was already angry and agitated. Tones of voices, eyes, gestures. English wasn't my first language, it was the tone underneath the tones of broken English, like poetry, one of the best reasons I always got slapped pointing this out, who I thought I was. There was a better way, but my sister didn't get through that either. C'mon, the big surprise as I got older, I got kinder. I cry at the stupidest human gesture. I fall madly in love with the woman who snorts when she laughs. Only, where I totally don't recognize myself is when I have to flunk one of my students without taking him aside and slapping him awake.

—Craig Czury

**You know, butt,** if you keep up the way you're going, you're gonna end up like that character over there, pointing to one of the strung-out, hungover guys on the street corner after our hair cuts, on our way to the Luzerne Legion where he'd prop me on a barstool in front of the pinball machine and feed me nickels all afternoon, not knowing I was racking up scores that kept my old man and his cronies in shot-n-beers all afternoon. This is my son the character, until a lot of years later, bucking hay bales up on the Montana Hi-line, carrying hod for bricklayers in the Nebraska badlands, cod slinging on the Oregon coast, pearl diving, fun-ride carny, minimum wage among guys who, with dignity, taught me that to have character is a high virtue. Your son with character. C'mon. What's it take to change your name and run away from home! I know I keep harping on this, but, strung-out and hungover, what's it take to have?

—*Craig Czury*

## *Space and Time*

*poems by Erin Delaney*

# Reflections on the Remains of the Ashley Coal Breaker

From this black rock
seeps the diamonds of our past.
This ever-burning stone
a historic smoke and mirror act of prosperity.
And when the ash was cleared,
it revealed an end
to the ancestry of our region,
a vein into our lifeblood:

abandoned coal crushers and factories,
those crumbled remains of
mid-day business,
thick, broken windows revealing
empty executive desks
with looseleaf expenditures
dated a century ago
smashed between the rubble-
and in the distance, the mine
is always open-

Its metal cart tracks
disappear into cavernous, dark depths
closing around a crouched path,
this crawlspace where great-grandfathers
tapped away twelve hours
pickaxe to craggy, lamplit walls
until the whistle of shift's end
gave way to immigrants pay
and dusty night-coughs in concrete cities-

It is a century's past that still consumes.
We- above the earthless spaces,
future generations of breaker boys,
releasing our broken spirits of ancestry,
mining our worlds to discover new diamonds.

—Erin Delaney

## Space and Time:  @StationCDRKelly

> *"Here, am I floating in my tin can far above the world. Planet Earth is blue and there's nothing I can do."*  —David Bowie

The space station passes overhead unblinking.
That floating tincan
encapsulated in a brief moment of moving light,
its quietude of space and time spinning always
reminds us a sun somewhere shines, reflects.
For a moment it beams, dashing across the night.
Then, as quickly as it appears,
it is bathed in darkness again
outside of eyesight, or horizon.

Somewhere out there,
below in the blue,
standing in our dewy grass patched coal field,
we remain.
Holding flashlights skyward,
we send up signals
captive to this thought:
Do they think of us as they pass overhead
spiraling above this world,
like a fleeting memory,
before fading back into invisible vantage points?

—Erin Delaney

# Thirst

Pennsylvania, the sunlight churns
heat beneath treetops and
water dries into snakelike
erosions in dirt.
No water for 16 miles.
The last source, a mirage
of fulfillment—
This small stream
salivates over
a fat dead mouse—
the trickling water
opens, gulps,
swallows its smelly corpse.

—*Erin Delaney*

## Mortality and the Uncut Rock

*for R. W. Emerson*

Below this uncut rock,
the mortal leaves
brown and crinkling
beneath this Sleepy Hollow
this dirt is sacred.
The earth moves and wriggles,
life within
stirs with anticipation.

R.W.'s fingernails
clawed this hallowed ground,
exhuming layers of rock and soil,
revealing gritty raw emotions
beneath its cool dark spaces.
Face to face with her decay-
life and death in its most raw form,
she remained a message to him,
a symbol of raw simplicity and inspiration.
His heartstrings mended,
communing with his Over-soul
as manicured grass stretching upward to the stars.

*—Erin Delaney*

*Transparency*
_____

*poems by Nancy Dymond*

# Transparency

Clean and clear;
they used to serve it
free at the Bluebird Diner
before we'd order
our steak and hash browns.

Chunks of it clunked
and clumped in
the eddy beyond the narrows.
Fish fucked in it.
Eagles fished in it.

Eels swam to its
source to spawn.
It sprinkled, tinkled
moistened, glazed
and fell as snow.

It cooled, heated
swelled and splashed.
it was a shape shifter.
it was clean.
it was clear.

They used to serve it—no charge.

*—Nancy Dymond*

# Under a Small Town: Two Conversations

A woman
another transplant to the area
like myself
sits beside me on the bench

You gotta live around here a long time, she says,
before you're one of them
I've been here 30 years

My mom and dad used to vacation here
I was just a kid skipping stones
on the lake - swimming, fishing

I bought a house here after I retired
Joined the garden club
Joined the local grange

Got to know the families
the Shecks, the Schwerks,
the Hanovers of Hanover Township

Being called a transplant is not an insult
I feel respected
People laugh politely at the label

I've noticed that the label
"transplant" or "import"
fades after 5 generations

But my kids' families
are all over the globe. My grandkids
think I've lived here forever

She's a Snyder? asks my sister-in-law,
Who's her father? Where does she live?
I hope she's not one of those Snyders
They're just not well thought of, that's all

Not from the area, I suspect
What church does she go to?
Lila Snyder was a Ramsey

Her mother used to
run the big factory downtown
while her dad was in the war

But those kids, that third generation
pulled the house down around them
killed the goose that laid the golden egg

Oh, that's no rumor
It was proved by DNA testing
"Uncle Daddy" got jobs for both sets of kids

Good jobs—they all stayed in the area
Most people's kids have to go away
to find work; good work, I mean

You're lucky here
You married into a good family
This family is well-connected

It's about character and connections
Who you know, who your family knows
Where you live, too

Ha! Their grandkids may
fit right in here someday
As proof of their pedigree

They'll point to my
slumping headstone
sitting crookedly
in the plot I purchased today.

    *—Nancy Dymond*

My grandmother ran
a boarding house for loggers
She was quite a cook

Have you seen our family headstone?
We have our names on it, no dates yet
If you want to
You can be buried there, too.

## Make New Friends

Even with eyes closed
She could see the place they were leaving
Eyes open she watched
A blurred landscape receding
Through the rear window
Of the family car

There goes the firehouse on Main Street
And the park behind it where
She and her sister won goldfish with
A well-aimed toss of a ping pong ball
There goes the brick elementary school
White circles for playing Dodge ball
Freshly painted on the asphalt
For the upcoming school year

She named her friends aloud as she
Saw their homes pass by
Tommy Hilbish, Deborah Longacre, Randy Kissinger
And her best friend Joyce Miller
All the time ringing in her mind were
The words of her parents
You'll make new friends, dear

She wondered if her parents would make new friends, too
Friends who would replace Lester Leister and his
Twin teenaged sons, Dean and Gene, who could sing
Hang Down Your Head Tom Dooley in harmony
Would they also replace Gerald and Adelaide Moyer
Who ate frog legs at the tavern on Saturday night
And who'd helped talk her parents into keeping
The stray dog that had followed her home one day?

The tall church steeple grew smaller above the trees
She could still see the very top of it
When they stopped for gas at the Esso station,
She turned in her seat and faced forward as
The aroma of gasoline
Spilled in through the open windows

    *—Nancy Dymond*

## Measured by Mercury

Seen from the bridge planks
over Skinner's Falls
the dark waters of the Delaware
display a charcoal sky of jagged clouds.
Ice floes clack against each other
in a journey measured by mercury
freezing down, melting up.

Irving Cliff rises above my town.
In the 1800s
the majestic Irving Hotel
lit up the skies as it
burned to the ground.

As if to memorialize
the grand spectacle
fireworks launch from the cliff
each Fourth of July.

January to June
July to December
each season presents its
pageant of opposing forces
with no two snowflakes
ever alike.

*—Nancy Dymond*

# *Night Music*

*poems by David Elliott*

## Again

Those ducks
startled and lifting

with so much
effort I almost

feel a pull into
the sky as if they

were rising right
through my body and

as they make it up
out of the water and fly

upstream I fall
back into

myself to catch
my breath

and inhabit this
dream again.

—*David Elliott*

## Through the Air

What is it that so moved me
about seeing two birds today
one a screech owl totally silent
body not moving head slightly rotating
attentive eyes—am I potential prey?—
and then that raptor gliding down
off a thermal toward me turning
into the sun its white head
shining bright the wingspan
immense—am I potential prey?—
seen for what I am a species
they must recover from
to grow more numerous again finding
their way to lift into the air we have
changed we have changed
the very air they fly through.

—*David Elliott*

## Rain in Nicholson

I can see from the window
it's raining in Nicholson.
It's always raining in Nicholson.
        Here
        hardly a trickle, the heat
        stubborn, a thug
        in love with his fist,
while up in Nicholson
clouds release gentle fingers
of rain...
    everywhere
    people helpless, bullied
    or caressed by fickle weather
    we can only talk about
forever.
The wind has shifted
as rain starts to pock the street.
        Could it be raining here
        but not in Nicholson?
Ridiculous!

    *—David Elliott*

## Climate

Temperature see-
saw, snow trending

shortsightedly,
global warming

stutter-fits, rain
to freeze, ice to thaw,

schizy climate, quick-
change artist, lawns

gone snow to grass
overnight, wind chill

reversals, some closed
eyes freezing shut.

*—David Elliott*

## Night Music

Cold winter night, lying in bed
reading, then pause,
resting the book on my chest...

tap dance of expanding
pipes, murmur of circulating
water, muffled roar
of the furnace heart deep
in the basement, tick
of a few snowflakes
on the windows...
                              closing
the book, taking off my glasses,
placing them on the bedside table
to see in the dark next to my head
all night,

all silent for now
not yet forever.

        —*David Elliott*

*Surviving Winter*
_____



*poems by Brian Fanelli*

## Outside a Scranton Deli, Talk of War

Waiter John puffs smokes on break,
leans against the brick wall,
checks his phone, scrolls for news—
another foiled ISIS plot.
*Those bastards are winning,* he says.
This is days after the Paris attacks,
American flags rippling in November wind,
hung from two-story Scranton homes,
where few could name Syria's capital,
but could list friends and siblings
who did three tours in Iraq.
I want to ask John about the *they*,
how *they're* winning. Here,
we lounge in diners, poke at eggs,
chatter about overseas bombings,
masked enemies we've seen
behead victims on YouTube.
Two hours away, the NYPD clench batons,
patrol Manhattan streets,
but still men and women in pea coats
sip their Starbucks, unfold their newspapers
before first shifts.
Here, John crushes his cigarette,
shakes his head, slips back to his shift,
jots down orders. I walk to my car,
blast the heat, complain about commercials
interrupting the news on my satellite radio.

—*Brian Fanelli*

## Evacuation

The governor and mayor, men safe in mansions,
lowered the evacuation notice to noon,
while my car inched towards home,
closer to National Guard tanks and flood zones,
where vans and pick-ups cut across side streets,
loaded with as much as a family could save
stuffed within four doors, the rest roof-strapped.
I pounded the wheel, cursed my decision to work
that morning, thinking the rain would ease, until I saw
I-81 resemble a doomsday movie—
rivers of cars honking horns, while the Susquehanna swelled.

Once home, I hugged you hard,
and like thieves, we ransacked our apartment,
pouring books, clothes, jewelry into boxes,
then raised furniture on milk crates,
while we whispered, *the levees will hold, the levees will hold.*
We shut all doors, locked all windows, feared
returning to warped floors, mud-caked walls.
We fled with what we could, whispered again,
*the levees will hold.*

For four days, we watched constant coverage—
homes swept from streets in Tunkhannock,
pushed downstream, smashed into bridges,
cars swallowed, towns without levees devoured.
Near our home, the river heaved against the dike,
fizzling and bubbling against white barriers
like soda leaking through a punctured can.

When we heard the order to return home,
the sun poked through clouds, first time
in days. This time, no tombstones or caskets
floated down the road from the Forty Fort Cemetery
like in '72. This time, our town's streets stayed dry,
homes as they had been left.

Months later, we biked along the dike,
gazed at chairs and clothes floating downstream,
a mud-slimed refrigerator caught in a tree,
others' misfortunes swallowed and spit out at the river's edge.

    *—Brian Fanelli*

## Autumn at Home

This year, trees burn slowly,
wisps of red and yellow
painted on a few leaves.

Last year you said,
*They blaze too quickly,*
*and all that remains is ash.*

Last fall, trees in our backyard
looked haunted and aged,
their twigs like crooked fingers.

Now I follow the Susquehanna's bend
along the river walk, where the sun sinks,
and the sky looks like a bruise.

A wind gust carries a few leaves to water,
where they float, crimson
near muddy banks.

I listen to branches creak,
watch them tremble like a pair of arms,
a body trying to pull tight its dress,

before what remains is stripped
by a force that builds each cooler week.

   *—Brian Fanelli*

## Surviving Winter

This winter almost killed me,
all those commutes down I-81,
clenching the wheel, white-knuckled,
sweating, while walls of snow flew off 18-wheelers
and my Hyundai trudged through ice.

When I arrived at class, lectured
before half-empty rooms, I realized
how little it mattered if I covered MLA
or reviewed Imagism for Friday's quiz
because we all gazed out the window,

watched sleet slick up roads,
cars swerve out of lanes,
while we waited for a text to tell us
evening classes would be canceled.

Now it is April, and the sky threatens rain.
Students huddle in libraries to finish final papers,
and I sigh when I walk on sidewalks and see
streaks of color against gray—
red and yellow tulips, crocuses sprouting
like green fingers rising from Earth.

Never have I needed summer as I do now,
after all those mornings squinting
through an ice-streaked windshield,
all those afternoons stuck behind plow trucks,
inching towards home on I-81,
closer to the semester's end.

*—Brian Fanelli*

## Steamtown Mall, Scranton

We called it downtown,
that colossal slab of concrete and stores,
that green Steamtown Mall sign
on Lackawanna Ave, beckoning consumers
like a lantern, a spark among closed warehouses
and empty brick buildings in nearby neighborhoods.

A boy, I clenched my dad's hand on opening weekend,
as shoppers bumped my shoulders, rushed
from store to store. We lingered outside the food court,
looked at the great locomotive rumbling
on nearby train tracks, its puffs of steam
rising in the air like cigarette smoke
from my dad's Marlboro.
*Progress,* he said. *This is progress.*

Now the mall is in foreclosure,
half the stores gated, while a few
stragglers wander like those scenes
in *Dawn of the Dead* when zombies
stumble around the shopping mall, groaning
next to department store mannequins
because they returned to what's familiar.

I recall my father's words, *This is Progress,*
and the images on local news of historic buildings
city officials pulverized for this block-long slab of stores.
The clouds of smoke and years of dust
rose up like a fist, while bulldozers roared.

      —*Brian Fanelli*

*Cold Comfort*
_____

*poems by Jane Julius Honchell*

# Expendable

Giants from some infernal fairy tale,
the breakers that crouched above the mines
of Olyphant and Carbondale to chew
black diamonds down to size had a dark
appetite for the blood of little boys.

Picture your own son—freckled third-grader,
Cub Scout, T-Ball player—as a breaker boy,
scarf pulled up against the dust that rises
like fog and settles everywhere, working ten-hour
shifts for fifty cents, breathing in that lethal air.

See your boy, bent-backed on a wooden seat
like a galley slave, thrust his boots into the ocean
of coal rumbling under his feet to slow it long
enough to pluck out rocks, clay, and the shards
of slate that cut bare hands to bloody ribbons.

Now imagine the worst: your rash, unwary lad
tumbling into that rough tide, sucked under, smothered
or minced to hash in the gear's sharp teeth. You won't know
he's gone until day's end, when they pull him out,
drop him at your door like a sack of trash.

*—Jane Julius Honchell*

## Travelers' Advisory

If you are a deer reading this,
first let me say: Stay away!
Don't cross the highway where
thickets cozy up to the road on both
sides of Route 6. It's an outdoor
abattoir for fawn and doe.

Just yesterday an SUV, glowing
like flame and big as a tank,
mowed down one of your own.
And mind you, she saw it coming,
picked up speed, bunched
her haunches for one last bound,
but the driver, with plenty of time
to stop, slammed her in mid-leap.
She flew in a russet arc, fell, slim legs
running crazily in place.
Phone still glued to an ear,
her killer never even slowed.

I tell you this because, despite
the havoc you wreak on my corn, scat
dropped on the patio, apples
poached from my trees, your large,
wild presence, just inches from my
window, makes me believe.

*—Jane Julius Honchell*

# Joy Ride

Flecks of pepper dotting the sky's cream, birds
rise and wheel in unison over the shopping
mall, K-Mart, cinema complex converted
to a church, Toys "R" Us and asphalted acres
planted with cars and rusty pickup trucks. Surely
some necessity compels their flight—
search for safe roost or food—but today
they seem to fly purely for their own amusement.

Staring out the restaurant window, spoon poised
between bowl and lips, I watch the flock do loop-
the-loops, barrel rolls and dives, flick back
and forth in tumbling Immelmann turns, split, regroup
into one great round—thousands of them—in a dance
so exuberant I watch until my soup grows cold.

*—Jane Julius Honchell*

# Cold Comfort

Five thousand miles from his Nigerian home,
my student shivers, flakes of his first
snow melting on the sharp obsidian planes
of his beautiful face. He's not sure
what to make of this soft white cold we natives
take in stride, bundled in warm jackets, scarves—
no sense of wonder—just the usual hunkering
down against another Northeast winter.

*In my country, it's the dry season now...
very hot,* he tells me, longing clear in his tone.
He's unprepared for a time when the sun
brings no heat. Only a thin hoodie stands
between his skin and this bitterness, so I'll give
him the old down coat my son abandoned
when he left home. I want to mother this boy, too,
fold him into the seasonless warmth we all call love.

      *—Jane Julius Honchell*

# *The Sharing*

*poems by Susan Luckstone Jaffer*

## Tara Hall

I raise my glass to darkened wood, to tin
Illuminations, gummy floor, and feet
That pound and spin in crazy unison.
From arms that fall across damp necks we meet
Eyes that laugh and tear with mirth so sweet
It turns our brittle cares to powder, blown
Out the door and down the weary street.
My music swells; we've made the tunes our own.
A beer is spilled, another dart is thrown.
And in the back, scrubbed table, seating shared,
Still seasick, homesick, wetly pale, half-grown,
Four young men paint their lyrics green. Unfair
Those WASPish weekdays keep me waiting long;
I'm turned to Irish with each Saturday's song.

*—Susan Luckstone Jaffer*

## Dream: February 12, 2002

An opaque night wind moves
gutter scraps soundlessly
around the curb. I am alone
on this unlit street corner, cold
black phone pressed to my ear,
but my voice has color.
I have been called to help.

A girl is telling me nervously
she's on the moon. She didn't know
the moon was so high. I ask
how she got there; she says
she doesn't know. She just started
climbing, and that's where she ended up.
She doesn't know how to get down.

As she talks, the moon is a silver
fragment with so much black sky
separating us that we seem to move
farther apart as I stare.

She gives me directions,
and I begin the upward
hike through rough brush
and over sand. It takes little time
to arrive at the moon—a grouping
of exhausted, splintered docks,
crumbling stone pilings.

Young people listless in discouraged
postures have given up looking
for a way down. I tell them I've been here
a thousand times, not knowing it was the moon.
They are silent in the face of my cheer.
Look, I tell them, it's a long drop; you can't
just jump feet first. You have to
use your whole body.

*Put your body into it,*
*my father told me, throwing a ball*
*when I was ten, blessedly unaware*
*of his only daughter's future*
*on and off the moon.*

I look down at rotted steps unable
to hold our weight. Explaining each move,
I turn to a concrete platform built on stone,
hard on my knees, painful under my hands
as I lower myself over its edge, praying
they will have the faith to follow.

I hang by my fingertips for just a second
before I let go and drop. It's a long fall, but I land
safely and awake in a room where sun warms
a jumble of clothes and the clock radio clicks
on. I sit up fast, listening hard, desperate to know
if I managed to save someone this time.

  *—Susan Luckstone Jaffer*

# The Visit

In the first rays of morning he opens
the kitchen door, letting in the cold
as he lets himself out. One hand pulls up
the brown corduroy collar of his worn canvas
jacket; the other guides the joystick. Down the ramp
and onto the grass. Frost crunches under his wheels.

Crisp white silence is broken by the soft hum
of the motor. He thinks of it as *his* motor now,
an internal force that begins with a thought and ends
where he wants to go. Each dawn this is his destination.

The house sleeps. Grey smoke rises in a thin plume
from the chimney. In a front bedroom, his wife
rolls cautiously onto her hip and pulls the comforter
around her shoulder. At her feet, a tabby stretches.
A mouse lies motionless in the attic.

Sun reaches sky now. Again he meets the challenge
of the road, a flat dirt ribbon once crossed in six strides.
He rounds the stone wall and heads down a slight incline
to the shed. In the first two bays, his faithful truck
and a long-grown son's once-red Camaro. In the third,
the tractor. His hand moves slowly back and forth
over the cracked rubber of the tire, eyes closing with a sigh.
When he opens them, his chair knows, and turns.
At the doorway of his barn, his love, he takes it in:
                pieces of rust
                        pieces of light.

    —Susan Luckstone Jaffer

# The Sharing

Emma Jean wonders if I have apples
to spare this year. My trees are laden. The grass is strewn
with early drops, bruised and dotted with rot, turning
our ankles, awaiting the eager mouths of deer.
Emma Jean has seen them. She knows I have no time
for Winesaps or Kings. She knows my days
of loading the trailer, heading out to the cider mill,
are over. But she asks, as if I'd somehow returned
to a time when autumn was more than a doorway to dog dishes
frozen to the ground, ice underfoot, bleak and impassable roads.

I have passed Emma Jean on this road for a quarter-century,
waved at her short-waisted figure in housedress and boots,
her community of cats, her tethered dog. She has been
to my house only twice. The first winter here, my second
daughter, weeks old, lay in her crib. Emma Jean thumped
to the door for stilted conversation, staying as my breasts filled
with milk. I willed my baby to stay asleep.

My second daughter lay in the morgue 25 years later.
Three days I waited for her to get up.
"I don't know how you feel," Emma Jean said then.
"I used to say I knew, but then Bob died,
and I realized no one knows."

Now she asks for apples. I pull them from low branches,
deep glossy red, mottled dull pink, rough yellow. They fall
into my bag as they will fall, sliced, into her pies,
constant despite everything.

The bag tied, I reach for a bowl. Outside, across the road
and through the gate, behind the barn, the hidden orchard,
once humming, stands silent with brown weeds and trunks
choked by poison ivy. In a jumble of branches a breeze
reveals plums: dusky purple in ripeness,
thinning skins slipping away, revealing pulp
at the slightest touch of my thumb.

—*Susan Luckstone Jaffer*

# A Pantoum for Gillian

*(1975 – 2001)*

The horses are gone now
What memories they leave
Whippoorwill Aurora:  the first light
Streaks of gold in the barnyard

What memories they leave
The Whippoorwill Morgans
Streaks of gold in the barnyard
Bays glistening in late-day sun

The Whippoorwill Morgans:
Such strength, such heart
Bays glistening in late-day sun
Everything my daughter wanted

Such strength, such heart
In a lovely young girl
Everything I wanted for her
And the woman she became.

In a lovely young girl's dream,
Her Morgans carried her,
And the woman she became,
Above fear, above pain.

Her Morgans carried her far.
What memories they leave
Above fear, above pain
The horses, gone now.

*—Susan Luckstone Jaffer*

*The River*

*poems by Dawn Leas*

## Susquehanna

She wakes too soon
       from winter's sleep
              not quite as angry as
                     four seasons ago
    when she flooded the private lives
of her neighbors. The same people
who year after year
                fight to save the beauty
    of her banks, defend
  her right to natural, slow-turning curves.
Her hair unravels in wild ribbons
of snowy ice as she roils
       against a man-made levee.
       She wants to spin her body like a supernova
across streets and fields, into homes, filling basements.
But wind gusts push her, and with the Chesapeake calling,
       she flows faster and faster.
       Horizontal lightning draws on a slate sky
           while thunder snow begins to fall,
     a scarred city and its scared people
     look to the southern horizon and shudder.

—*Dawn Leas*

## The River

embraces her body at any shape
flaunts blemishes on banks
when levels are low,
revels in rocking the levee
with wild hips,

waits for a dare
to lavish the valley
with her love
again and again and again.

*—Dawn Leas*

# A Lesson on Resilience

*Summer 2006*

The Lackawanna rises.

    For attention, little sister cries
    muddy water for big sister

The Susquehanna fills.

    who releases gates in sibling
    solitude of purpose.

Toby's Creek swells.

    Sky beats earth soft, malleable
    in its twisted artisan's hands,
    opened its eyes wide to truth.
    Weeping for days, sadness pools
    lake, river, stream and creek…

Huntsville Dam weakens.

    cajoling step cousins to swim together
    inside (and out) an uncontrolled
    common bank. Meanwhile

Anthracite Country screams.

    an old mine yawns torrents of water
    on a shocked hill town. Roads stripped
    to brick underclothing crumble.

Not again. Not again.

    River weeps streams tracing a line of history-
    jagged, selfish, defiant. Trees twist
    for a better view and white caps toss lost
    branches toward a resting place of sludge,
    debris and haunting Agnes memories.

    —*Dawn Leas*

## Independence

The rain comes every day for weeks. Sometimes in giant bursts, droplets breaking on tree branches. Often in drenching curtains, the wind blows west to east. The water pools muddied in the construction site outside my office. I'm quickly giving up on summer. You're saying you'll never let go. On the eve of the fourth of July, it's dry. We drive over an hour to the middle of nowhere for a softball game. There's a tractor parked outside the Turbotville Great Valu and marked spots for buggies. A young couple climbs into one. He's suspendered and bearded. She's white-capped and long-dressed, unwrinkled. They look full of hope. I think there's a poem here. I try to take pictures, but my memory is full. You refrain from a lecture. My niece throws strike after strike after strike in the bottom of the sixth. The stands cheer. The next day we wake to more rain.

—*Dawn Leas*

## Storm Front

Blue sky sours to green
and black. Iridescent
lightning zaps peak,
vibrates rock, runs
through veins
of the mountain
to water. The hum
of electricity
skitters across pond's
surface. Ripples speak.
Silence of summer breaks.

*—Dawn Leas*

*Stages of Forgiveness*
_____

*poems by Laurel Radzieski*

## Mine Story I

Vines grew within the rock. Men would blast sections of wall, then sift the coal for black leaves and dirty fruit. Several tunnels featured chandeliers of stems and branches, occasional root tapestries. Some vines were silky to the touch, others were prickly and bled heavily when cut.

—*Laurel Radzieski*

## Mine Story II

On rare occasions, the floor of a tunnel caved in, depositing a surprised miner, mule and cart in an underground lake. Miners were instructed to remain still after a fall, but most began thrashing and were eaten quickly by various creatures. When a man (or what remained of him) was rescued, a temporary bridge was erected across the chasm. Some miners took to fishing before or after shifts. Most tossed debris into the lakes, hoping to fill them.

*—Laurel Radzieski*

## Mine Story III

Boys and men in the mines could taste the groan of shifting rock, the creak of strained wood. Some men could hear a rat in terror three rooms away. As the mine shifted, so did the rats. Their features disgusted and fascinated William. He studied their thick tails and lice-ridden ears, the black oval eyes that spread to their foreheads. Grotesque and seemingly pupil-less, the eyes appeared ready to burst. William did not feed the rats like the other men did, though he often followed their departures. More than the mountain, the men trusted the rats.

—*Laurel Radzieski*

## Stages of Forgiveness

I followed my father's shadow
into the mountain
though he did not ask me to.
He went first, for, in many cases,
I am slow and heavy.

The mountain was a he,
but the mines with their tunnels,
rocks and earth,
these are always female.

When my father died
we sawed off his antlers
and tied them above the door

to make our house larger
than the other houses.

—*Laurel Radzieski*

*Acknowledgments*

We would like to acknowledge our appreciation to the editors of the venues where some of the works in this anthology first appeared.

David Elliott

"Rain in Nicholson" was first published in *Got Verse: an Anthology of Valley Poetry* by New American Press, 2002

Brian Fanelli

"Evacuation" was first published in his book *All That Remains* by Unbound Content, 2013.

Susan Luckstone Jaffer

"The Visit" was part of a collaboration between the Northeast Photography Club and local writers presented as a juried exhibit at Marywood University and published in a catalog of that exhibit.

Dawn Leas

"A Lesson on Resilience" was first published in *Word Fountain,* Special Flood Issue, 2012.

"Susquehanna" first appeared in the Umbrella Project curated by Nicelle Davis for the Association of Writers and Writing Programs' 2014 conference in Seattle.

*About the Authors*

**Thomas Kielty Blomain** is a writer of poetry, stories, and songs. Author of *Gray Area* (Nightshade Press), *Blues From Paradise* (Foothills Publishing), and *Yellow Trophies* (NYQ Books), he served as editor of *5 Poets* (Nightshade Press), and has had a longtime affiliation with Scranton-based Mulberry Poets and Writers Association. A reasonably good guitar player and singer, he occasionally co-produces *Graffiti,* an eclectic poetry and music show for Electric City Television. A graduate of Keystone Junior College and Dickinson College, he holds professional designations in underwriting and consulting from The American College and works in the insurance field. He resides in Scranton's Hill Scranton with his wife, Jessica. Author photo by Jessica Blomain.

**Amanda J. Bradley** has published two poetry books with NYQ Books, *Oz at Night* (2011) and *Hints and Allegations* (2009). Her poems and essays have appeared in *Rattle, Gargoyle, Paterson Literary Review, The Nervous Breakdown,* and *Kin Poetry Journal,* among many others. She earned a PhD from Washington University in Saint Louis in English and American Literature and an MFA in Poetry Writing from The New School in Manhattan. She teaches literature and creative writing at Keystone College in La Plume, PA, outside of Scranton. Author photo by Brian Adams. www.amandajbradley.com

**Craig Czury** (Creative Writing MFA, Wilkes University) has spent three decades conducting poetry, life-writing, and writing as healing workshops in schools, universities, community centers, prisons, homeless shelters, and mental hospitals. A lecturer at Albright University, editor, publisher, and tireless arts activist, Craig is the author of over 20 books of poetry, most recently *Thumb Notes Almanac: Hitchhiking The Marcellus Shale,* a poetry documentary woven from his hitchhiking interviews and observations while hitchhiking through the heart of "fracking" in his home region of Northeastern Pennsylvania. He is the co-host and artistic director of The Old School Poetry Series at The Springville Schoolhouse Art Studios in Susquehanna County, where he lives, works and plays bocce. Author photo by Pamela Daza. www.craigczury.com

*113*

**Erin L. Delaney** is a digital content and product copywriter who loves trekking the mountains of NEPA, taking photos for Instagram, blogging and writing poetry. She has written articles for *EZineArticles.com, The EC/DC, The Women's Newspaper,* and *Philadelphia City Paper.* Her poetry has been published with *Instress Magazine,* the Luzerne County Transit Authority's Poetry-in-Transit program, Paper Kite Press, and has been featured at numerous venues along the East Coast. She has an MA in Nonfiction and Poetry from Wilkes University and resides with her husband, Aaron, and two sons, Sebastian and Silas. erindelaney.wordpress.com

**Nancy Dymond** is a poet, playwright, aspiring actor and freelance writer. Her freelance work and occasional poetry have appeared in *The Milford Journal, The River Reporter Newspaper, Clever Girl Magazine, Wayne Independent Newspaper,* online at *Right Hand Pointing,* and in several anthologies produced by the Upper Delaware Writers Collective. Several of her poems have received recognition in college competitions, winning first and second place awards for two consecutive years in the Alyssa Katon Writing Contest. Her poem, "The Road To Night," won first place in the 2011 Mulberry Poets & Writers Regional Poetry Contest. In 2015 her first volume of poetry, *Sleep Barn,* was published by Stockport Flats Press of New Paltz, New York.

**David Elliott** is Professor Emeritus at Keystone College where he taught creative writing, literature, composition, and jazz history courses. He is the author of two books of poetry: *Wind in the Trees* and *Passing Through.* His poetry has also appeared in several anthologies, including *Haiku in English: The First Hundred Years* and *The Haiku Anthology,* both published by W.W. Norton, *Got Verse: Valley Poetry Anthology,* and *Palpable Clock: 25 Years of Mulberry Poets.* For many years he served on the Board of the Mulberry Poets and Writers Association.

**Brian Fanelli** is the author of *Front Man* (Big Table Publishing), *All That Remains* (Unbound Content), and *Waiting for the Dead to Speak* (NYQ Books). His poetry, essays, and book reviews have been published by *The Los Angeles Times, World Literature Today, The Paterson Literary Review, Main Street Rag, [PANK], Kentucky Review, Stone Canoe,* and elsewhere. He has an MFA from Wilkes University and a PhD from Binghamton University. He is a professor of English at Lackawanna College. Author photo by Daryl Sznyter. www.brianfanelli.com

**Jane Julius Honchell** is an Associate Professor in the School of Arts and Sciences at Keystone College, and a former staff feature writer and columnist with *The Scranton Times.* Jane is the author of three prize-winning plays, and her poetry has appeared in *Palpable Clock: 25 Years of Mulberry Poets* and *Five Poets.* She has been a Mulberry Poets featured reader and has participated in WVIA-FM's "Poetry Minutes" series. Her first book of poetry, *A Satisfactory Daughter,* will be published by NYQ Books. She is the mother of Amy and Bill and lives in Glenburn, PA. Author photo by Kassidy Evans Kraky.

**Susan Luckstone Jaffer's** poetry has appeared in *America, Yankee, Light,* and *The Lyric,* among others. Three of her poems appeared in the book *Palpable Clock: 25 Years of Mulberry Poets*, published by the University of Scranton. Originally from New York City, Susan raised her family on an old farm in Northeast Pennsylvania and lives there still.

**Dawn Leas's** work has appeared in *Literary Mama, San Pedro River Review, Connecticut River Review, The Pedestal Magazine,* and elsewhere. Her chapbook, *I Know When to Keep Quiet,* was published by Finishing Line Press (2010). A collection of her poems can be found in *Everyday Escape Poems,* an anthology released by SwanDive Publishing (2014), and her first full-length collection, *Take Something When You Go,* was published in April 2016 by Winter Goose Publishing. She earned an MFA in Creative Writing from Wilkes University where she is currently assistant to the president. She is also a contributing editor at *Poets' Quarterly* and *THEthe Poetry.* Author photo by Nathan Summerlin. www.dawnleas.com

**Laurel Radzieski** is an MFA graduate of Goddard College who spends her days working on nonprofit endeavors. She is a poetry editor for *Clockhouse* and her work has appeared in *Really System, inkscrawl, Story* and *The Same.* Her poetry has also been featured on the Farm/Art DTour in Sauk County, WI. Author photo by Pat Henneforth.

Nightshade Press was established by Carolyn Page and Roy Zarucchi in Troy, ME in 1989. While in Maine, Page and Zarucchi published over 75 poetry and prose titles. They also published 19 editions of a magazine called *Potato Eyes*. In 2003, Karen Blomain, a professor at Keystone College and one of the first poets published by Nightshade, arranged for Keystone to purchase Nightshade Press. In 2016, after a brief hiatus, Keystone College President David Coppola asked Ray Hammond to re-invigorate the press with an emphasis on student involvement.